CW00869535

CONTENTS

IN THE BEGINNING

by Colin Lancashire M.Sc. Dip.Ed.

In The Beginning
ISBN 1-902370-06-6

Published by
EMMAUS BIBLE SCHOOL U.K.

1st Printing - May 2000

Printed by
EMMAUS BIBLE SCHOOL U.K.
Carlett Boulevard, Eastham, Wirral CH62 8BZ
Tel: 0151 327 1172 Fax: 0151 327 1592

INSTRUCTIONS TO STUDENTS

HOW TO STUDY
Begin by asking God to open your heart to receive the truths He would teach you from His Word. Read the lesson through at least twice, once to get an overall view of its contents and then again, slowly, looking up all Scripture references, for these are the most important parts of the course.

EXAMS
Enter your name and address at the top of each exam paper and then complete each of the questions, using extra paper for your answers if required. Please also indicate which version of the Bible you have used. Your tutor will mark all your answers and for those which are incorrect, he/she will refer you to the place in the Bible or the textbook where the correct answer is found to enable you to check it again for yourself?

WHAT DO YOU THINK?
In the final part you may freely state your own views on the whole or any part of this course. This will enable your tutor to understand your thinking and will help us to evaluate the general response and effectiveness of this course.

TIME LIMIT
The School places no actual limit on your studies which allows you to proceed at your own pace. We do, however, strongly recommend that you keep to a regular schedule, for in this way the maximum benefit is attained.

Please send the exam paper only, after cutting it out of the book, together with a suitable , stamped addressed envelope for the return of your corrected paper. Thank you.

INTRODUCTION

The issues addressed in this course are fundamental and basic to the Christian faith for they concern the authority and reliability of what God has said and recorded in the scriptures, especially in the opening chapters.

Popular science is regarded by many today as having dealt a death blow to the Biblical account of creation and if this is true then the whole of scripture would have fallen with it for the Bible is one complete book in which every part is interrelated and every truth interwoven.

This course presents a basic introduction to some of the issues of evolution and creation and is intended to show students that the Biblical account of origins is in perfect agreement with the facts of true science, for both belong to God.

There are many claims and counter-claims put forward from different areas and perceptions of science which are outside the scope and intention of this course. Students who wish to look into these issues in greater depth will find many helpful sources available, some of which are detailed at the end of this book.

The student is urged to follow up every scripture reference and to carefully and prayerfully consider the issues presented in order to arrive at the truth God wants us to know.

Thou, even thou, art LORD alone; thou hast made heaven, the heaven of heavens, with all their host, the earth, and all things that are therein, the seas, and all that is therein, and thou preservest them all; and the host of heaven worshippeth thee.

Nehemiah 9.6

God, who made the world and everything in it, since He is Lord of heaven and earth, does not dwell in temples made with hands. Nor is He worshiped with men's hands, as though He needed anything, since He gives to all life, breath, and all things. And He has made from one blood every nation of men to dwell on all the face of the earth, and has determined their preappointed times and the boundaries of their dwellings.

Acts 17.24 - 26 NKJV

LESSON 1

A FOUNDATION FOR BELIEF

We all have a basis or starting point for our thinking and beliefs which depends largely on our past experience and present knowledge. Everyone of us, whether we realize it or not, have pre-suppositions which influence what we believe and the way that we live. Our beliefs regarding origin, purpose and destiny are of the utmost importance and demand a careful examination of the foundation upon which they are built.

When looking for an explanation of the world around us there are two basic starting points or models; one is evolutionary or naturalistic, and the other is creational or supernatural. These two world views lead to different conclusions, so that it is essential to consider the nature of each and to examine the principles on which they are based, for the foundation on which we build will determine our whole understanding and attitude to life.

First we need to define what is meant by 'evolution' and 'creation', so that we clearly understand the issues with which we are dealing. Biological evolution, in broad terms, refers to changes in the genetic structure of organisms over the passage of time. Essentially this must be divided into microevolution and macroevolution.

Microevolution involves minor changes in organisms over short periods of time which have been, and can be, observed. Macroevolution involves major transformations of organisms over vast periods of time, and it is seen by many as the mechanism which links all living things in a chain of descent to a common ancestor, although this has never been, nor could be, observed. In this course the term 'evolution', will be used in the sense of macroevolution, unless stated otherwise.

Creation, in broad terms, refers to the original, initial work of God in bringing materials into being which were previously non-existent in any form, and then setting up the universe from these basic materials.

Evolution, like Christianity, is not a science, it is a philosophy, a belief system, and to some it seems, a religion adhered to with great fervour. Neither of these two beliefs can be tested by any scientific method but have to be accepted by faith. None of the processes involved in evolution or creation are observable, measurable or repeatable and cannot, therefore, be subjected to any experimental method to prove their validity.

Evolution is linked with uniformitarianism - the concept that geological processes such as erosion and sedimentation have remained almost constant in character and rate over long periods of time. The underlying belief here is that the present is the key to the past - what is happening now is what has always happened. Creationism, or Biblical science, recognises slow, natural processes but also the occurrence and very significant contribution of sudden catastrophic events, notably the earth changes set in motion by the global flood in Noah's time and other acts of divine intervention as recorded in the Old and New Testaments. (eg. Genesis 19.24-26, Exodus14.21, Luke 1.34/35 Matthew 27.51-53)

Evolutionists see the universe as a self-determining and self-regulating natural system, so that all events and phenomenon are explained in terms of the factors within that system. Creationists recognise that outside of this system there is an all-powerful and all-intelligent God who has designed and who maintains the universe according to His own purposes. This is the most fundamental difference between the two beliefs.

There is a lot of literature available dealing with origins from an evolutionary perspective because this theory is almost the only one taught and accepted today in centres of education and throughout the media. The approach in this course is to show that the true facts of science fit readily into a biblical framework and that together they present a harmonious and meaningful account of origin, purpose and destiny. If you have never looked into the Bible for answers to questions about yourself and the world around you, we would ask you to carefully consider the following pages and to read God's Word for yourself and give Him the opportunity to speak to you through it.

The accuracy and authority of the Word of God is the basis for belief in this, and every other, Emmaus course. God's revelation is the only totally reliable source of knowledge for without this man is left to arrange and re-arrange his own knowledge or ignorance according to his perception and evaluation of himself and his surroundings.

Science needs a sound basis or background for accurate and reliable interpretation and this sound basis is the Word of God. The theories of evolutionists need to be continually modified, and in many cases should be abandoned altogether, but knowledge based on scripture has proved to be trustworthy and able to stand the test of time. Christians, who believe in the authority and accuracy of the Word of God, are able to make the bold assertion that no fact discovered by science will ever be proved to contradict scripture. There are two ways, therefore, in which the claims of evolutionary theory can be answered - one is through a correct interpretation of Scripture and the other is through a correct interpretation of science, both of which will be found to be in complete agreement with one another for God is the Originator of both.

The safe and sure ground for the Christian is to recognise the reliability of scripture and to use it to form a broad foundation and framework for scientific interpretation. The God we have trusted for eternal salvation can be depended on to tell us the truth about how everything began and how everything will end. The Lord Jesus said, 'I am Alpha and Omega, the beginning and the ending, saith the Lord, which is, and which was, and which is to come, the Almighty' (Revelation 1.8).

A fundamental difference between a Christian approach and a non-Christian approach is seen in the value that is placed on the Word of God. According to scripture, faith is the essential ingredient to the understanding of those things that cannot be subjected to scientific proof.

The Bible teaches that it is -

' through faith we understand (intelligently discern) that the worlds (the universe and the ages of time) were framed (made perfect or completed) by the word (spoken word) of God' (Hebrews 11.3).

Furthermore -
'he that cometh to God must believe that he is (exists) and that he is a rewarder of them that diligently seek him' (Hebrews 11.6).

The key to knowledge and understanding comes from a recognition of the existence of God and an acknowledgement of what He has done. In Romans we read, 'the invisible things of him from the creation of the world are clearly seen, being understood by the things that are made, even his eternal power and Godhead; so that they are without excuse' (Romans 1.20).

The God who cannot be seen has made Himself known through that which can be seen and experienced. The evidence for the existence of God is around us and within us for the voices of creation and conscience clearly convey a sense of our dependence on Him and our accountability to Him. This is largely why man seems so desperate to find alternative explanations for the world around us, but he remains without excuse for his ignorance. The major flaw in popular evolutionary theory, even though plausibly presented, is that it has no room for God.

We must approach science through the enlightenment of scripture rather than come to conclusions about scripture through the eyes of popular science. Christians must read and interpret the Word of God without being influenced by what the philosophies of men require them to believe. Let the Bible speak for itself and let us build our faith on what it reveals, for the authority of the Bible is the authority of God. It has stood the tests of time with dignity and strength, towering majestically above the wrecks of human belief systems.

We should explore and expound scripture first and then seek to understand the world through what God has revealed, for science does not belong to scientists, it belongs to God.

LESSON 2

AN INTRODUCTION TO GENESIS

Genesis is the book of beginnings; it is the book in which foundations are laid both for God's Word and for God's World. This first book in the Bible is the foundation for all the other books; the first chapter in the Bible is the foundation for the first book and the first verse in the Bible is the foundation for the first chapter.

A foundation must be sound and immoveable otherwise what is built on it will also prove to be unreliable and unstable. The opening verses of God's book are most important, for if the first few pages are untrue or misleading we can have little confidence in the rest.

Another important truth to grasp is that the Bible is self-supporting, that is, statements made in one part are frequently referred to and confirmed in other parts, and it is these interwoven links which hold the whole book together. In this course numerous other scripture verses will be appealed to for the light they shed on seeming difficulties in the account of creation.

There are around 150 references or allusions to Genesis in the rest of the Old Testament and about 200 in the New Testament. Nearly every other book in the Bible either quotes from Genesis or refers to it in some way. The New Testament refers to Genesis 1.1 - 2.3. twenty four times, verifying its accuracy and confirming the foundation on which the whole superstructure of divine revelation rests.

Genesis sets the scene for the unfolding drama of human history. It is the seed plot of the Bible in which many seeds are planted deep and do not come to fruition for some time. (eg 3.15, 8.22, 12.2/3, 49.10.). It is not a book of myths, half truths, legends or stories just for children, but is an accurate and reliable history of real events and real people. The Lord Jesus refers to Adam, Eve, Abel, Noah, Abraham, Lot, Isaac, Jacob, Moses and also to Sodom and Gomorrah. He underlines the authority of the books of Moses by saying, 'if you do not believe his writings, how will you believe My words' (John 5.47NKJV). In none of these New Testament references is there the slightest indication that the events or persons mentioned are to be regarded as mythological or allegorical, but historical and literal. God does not build truths on myths but on facts.

Genesis chapter one is historical narrative and consists of a straightforward, factual account of origins. It contains details unknowable apart from divine revelation and it stands in contrast to the stories of beginnings handed down from many other civilisations. These other accounts of how the world began indicate a common origin for there are certain elements in them which are reflections of the truth which God has revealed to man, but the first chapter of Genesis is a unique piece of literature that far exceeds any other that comes from the ancient or modern world. Genesis records literal history with oral and written information preserved and passed down through generations.

On ten occasions in Genesis* we read, 'these are the generations (or accounts) of' ; indicating that what follows was recorded by the person, or persons, named, then handed down to succeeding generations and finally brought together by Moses, under the inspiration of the Holy Spirit, for inclusion in scripture (2 Peter 1.21). The importance of Genesis is further seen in that this first book of the Bible covers a period of about 2,300 years, which is more than one third of human history.

In Genesis 1.1 to 2.3 we are presented with the framework or outline, of God's creative activity. Much detail is omitted as non-essential in

* 2.4; 5.1; 6.9; 10.1; 11.10,27; 25.12,19; 36.1,9; 37.2

this divine narrative, which means that not all of our questions are answered nor will our curiosity always be satisfied. What we are given is like all the edge pieces of a jigsaw puzzle which form the outline of the whole picture into which every other piece will be seen to fit.

The whole truth has not been fully revealed to us as yet, but there are guidelines drawn in scripture within which we must stay. These limiting factors are defined and understood by drawing on the whole of the Word of God, which, when accurately translated and correctly interpreted, provide us with all God wants us to know now.

The purpose of this opening chapter of the Bible is to show the progression of events that led up to the creation of man. God has not given us all the details on the first page of His book, so this leaves room for further development in scripture and further discovery by science. These will be seen to be in harmony with each other, for God is the Designer of both. True science and scripture are complementary not contradictory, for God's WORLD is not at odds with God's WORD. When honest and accurate conclusions are drawn from scientific data these can (or eventually will) be shown to fit into a biblical framework. It has to be stressed that Christians do not yet know all the answers but if our foundations are right we are well on the way to finding true explanations.

The Genesis record provides us with a continuous account of creation. The first word in every verse, from verse two onwards, can be translated 'and', which indicates that each statement is sequential and is chronologically connected to verses before and after. The events described are intended to be understood as having taken place in close succession throughout the creation week.

In the opening statement of the Bible, God introduces Himself as the One who works powerfully, systematically and purposefully in creation.

The eternal will of God is to be accomplished through time ages and this is the point at which Genesis begins. Here God steps out of the vast, timeless eternity and in a magnificent display of divine intelligence and power, He creates a world consisting of time, energy, space and matter. He starts with the framework of the universe, forming the earth as the centre of activity and developing it to sustain life which He goes on to create in all its variety. His crowning work is the creation of man in His own image and likeness and for His own purpose and pleasure. In Revelation 4.11 we read,

'Thou art worthy, O Lord, to receive glory and honour and power for thou hast created all things and for thy pleasure (will) they are (exist) and were created.'

It is important to see that God works in progressive stages. He does not produce the finished work of creation in one instantaneous operation but He works to a plan through which we are introduced to divine principles in action. This plan can be summarised in five stages as follows -

Stage 1. THE EARTH IS PRODUCED (v1-2) - its creation.
Materials are brought into existence and foundations are laid.

Stage 2. THE EARTH IS PREPARED (v3-10) - its construction.
Materials are organised and structures put together.

Stage 3. THE EARTH IS PROGRAMMED (v11-19) - its continuation.
Food and seasons are introduced for the sustaining of ordered life.

Stage 4. THE EARTH IS POPULATED (v20-25) - its classification.
A whole variety of animal life fills the sea, sky and land.

Stage 5. THE EARTH IS POSSESSED (v26 - 2.3) - its completion.
Man, God's masterpiece, is placed on earth as head of God's creation.

A built-in division of the creation record is provided by the events of each day.

> Day One v3-5 Light divided from darkness
>
> Day Two v6-8 Waters divided by the sky
>
> Day Three v9-13 Sea, land and vegetation
>
> Day Four v14-19 Lights in the heaven
>
> Day Five v20-23 Life in the sea and sky
>
> Day Six v24-31 Life on land including Man
>
> Day Seven v2.1-3 God's rest through completion

In four simplified stages we see the Earth -
Founded (v1-5), Formed (v6-10), Filled (v11-31) and Finished (2.1-3).

It is very interesting and instructive to observe how God's creative work fits within a timescale of seven days. Seven is a significant number in scripture, for it is the number of completion and when used of God's work it indicates perfect completion. Along with other numbers it serves as a divine signature linking together the work of God throughout the whole of scripture. Here, for example, the seven day cycle not only serves as a continual reminder of God's creation week, but it establishes a basis for work and rest that man neglects at his own cost. (Read Leviticus 25 for more cycles of seven.)

LESSON 3

THE FIRST STATEMENT OF SCRIPTURE

Genesis 1.1 'In the beginning God created the heavens and the earth'.

Genesis begins with God, but God does not begin in Genesis. He has no beginning and no end and therefore He is not a part of the world process. Everything else has a beginning - only God is eternal. He is described in the New Testament as, 'eternal, immortal, invisible, the only wise God' (1 Timothy 1.17), 'dwelling in the light which no man can approach unto; whom no man hath seen, nor can see' (1 Timothy 6.16). (Read Psalm 90.2)

This opening statement refers to the beginning of time not of eternity, for eternity has neither beginning nor end; it is the beginning of the created not the Creator. Here is the absolute beginning in which God willed the existence of that which formerly had no existence. God is the Creator of all things and this great truth is the key to understanding the meaning of life.

This first verse can be compared with John 1.1-4 where we read -

'In the beginning was the Word, and the Word was with God, and the Word was God. He was in the beginning with God. All things were made through Him, and without Him nothing was made that was made. In Him was life, and the life was the light of men.' (NKJV)

The 'beginning' here is the same as that in the first verse of Genesis - that is, the point at which creation began.

Note what the scripture teaches about Christ as the Son of God -

1. He created everything therefore He Himself is uncreated.

2. Because He is uncreated He must be eternal.

3. Because He is eternal He must be God.

The Son of God is called the Word, for He is the One who completely communicates all that God is and has done. But as well as communication, the Word speaks of information, an enormous amount of which was put into the creation process. In this the Son was active for we read that it was through Him God made the worlds, (Hebrews 1.2). Another scripture speaks of God, creating all things by Jesus Christ (Ephesians 3.9).

In Colossians 1.16-17 we read -
'by him were all things created, that are in heaven, and that are in earth, visible and invisible, whether they be thrones, or dominions, or principalities, or powers: all things were created by him, and for him. And he is before all things, and by him all things consist.'

Truth of this magnitude could never be accessed and appreciated through evolutionary theory or through any search that originated from man, but only as the result of divine revelation, and this is why the Word of God is far superior to the belief systems of men.

This opening sentence is very important and significant for -
1. 'In the beginning' - GOD PRESENTS TIME - the clock of the universe starts to tick as the eternal God begins to build an ordered system with a limited duration. A divine chronology is established not only for the initial creation but also for the unfolding ages of time.
2. 'God created' - GOD PROVIDES ENERGY - an unlimited source of divine power brings this time system into existence and subsequently keeps it going.
3. 'the heavens' - GOD PREPARES SPACE - He determines the bounds within which the universe exists; a seemingly unlimited expanse in which all creation is contained.

4. 'and the earth' - GOD PRODUCES MATTER - the material of which all things are made. Matter has mass and occupies space in time.

So we have -   1. TIME - during which things happen.
                2. ENERGY - through which work is done
                3. SPACE - in which the universe exists
                4. MATTER - of which everything is made.

Energy, space and matter can only exist in time for they are changeable and change belongs to time. God created all these but He Himself is not dependent on them or subject to the conditions and laws which govern them. Being eternal, God is not dependent on the things that belong to time.

So in this first verse of the Bible -
God composes time, but He is outside of it and cannot be confined to it.
God controls energy, but He is not subject to it or dependent on it.
God confines space, but He is outside of it and cannot be contained within it.
God creates matter, but He does not consist of it for He is Spirit
(Read 1 Kings 8.27; Psalm 90.4; Isaiah 40.28; 57.15; Malachi 3.6; John 4.24)

Yet as we read on into the New Testament we find that in the Person of the LORD JESUS CHRIST, God came within all these bounds, not as a bystander but as a participant, causing Paul to write, 'great is the mystery of godliness: God was manifest in the flesh ...' (1 Timothy 3:16; Hebrews 2.14). The Son of God, the Creator, willingly came inside these limitations and submitted Himself to them. He made Himself subject to human conditions by entering the human race, experiencing life as we do, with this great exception that although He became the bearer of the sin of the world (John 1.29). He Himself was totally without sin (2 Corinthians 5.21, 1Peter 2.22, 1John 3.5).

The heavens are mentioned before the earth which seems to indicate that they were first in order of creation. Perhaps, therefore, we are to understand that this included the host of angels, the 'sons of God' who witnessed the rest of God's work, (Job 38.7). It is possible that the angels are included in the ' hosts ' of Genesis 2.1. At the birth of Christ 'the heavenly host' of angels were there to witness an even greater work of God (Luke 2.13). The Psalmist says, 'By the word of the Lord were the heavens made; and all the host of them by the breath of his mouth' (Psalm 33.6).

The foundations are thus laid for the ' first heaven and the first earth' (Revelation 21.1) from the materials God has created. Several other scriptures confirm this first, foundational work of God.

'Of old hast thou **laid the foundation** of the earth: and the heavens are the work of thy hands' (Psalm 102:25).
'Mine hand also hath **laid the foundation** of the earth, and my right hand hath spanned the heavens: when I call unto them, they stand up together' (Isaiah 48:13).
'the LORD, which stretcheth forth the heavens, and **layeth the foundation** of the earth, and formeth the spirit of man within him' (Zechariah 12:1).

The foundations of a work are always associated with its beginning, so also with God's work. But when was this beginning? We find that numbers, dates and times feature largely in the Old Testament for God frequently links specific events to a point or period of time. It is thus possible to construct a complete chronology from biblical data, not only for the book of Genesis but also for the whole of the Old Testament.

A Table like the one shown below can provide interesting, and perhaps unexpected, information. It shows, for example, that the time covered by the book of Genesis is spanned by the lives of five men - Adam, Lamech, Shem, Isaac and Joseph, with each being contemporary with the next for at least 29 years, thus facilitating the passing on of historical information. Using this chronology and calculating back from the Exodus gives a date of 4174 BC for the creation of Adam.

A Chronology from Adam to Jacob

	Year from Adam	Age at birth of son	Age at death	Year of death
Adam	0	130	930	930
Seth	130	105	912	1042
Enos	235	90	905	1140
Cainan	325	70	910	1235
Mahalalel	395	65	895	1290
Jared	460	162	962	1422
Enoch	622	65	365	987 (translated)
Methuselah	687	187	969	1656
Lamech	874	182	777	1651
Noah	1056	502	950	2006
Shem	1558	100	600	2158
Arphaxad	1658	35	438	2096
Salah	1693	30	433	2126
Eber	1723	34	464	2187
Peleg	1757	30	239	1996
Reu	1787	32	239	2026
Serug	1819	30	230	2049
Nahor	1849	29	148	1997
Terah	1878	130	205	2083
Abraham	2008	100	175	2183
Isaac	2108	60	180	2288
Jacob	2168	91	147	2315
Joseph	2259	-	110	2369
To Egypt	2298			
Exodus	2728 (1446 B.C.)			

Temple begun 3207 (967 B.C.) See 1 Kings 6.1

There is no sound reason why a time scale like this should be rejected, either from within scripture itself or from the requirements of God's scientific work.

All actual, historical records agree in substance with the short chronology of the Bible. Many people reject dates, like that given by Ussher*, of around 4000 B.C. for the creation, but Sir Isaac Newton and his contemporaries accepted this implicitly. In the 17th and 18th centuries any suggestion that human history extended back beyond 6000 years was considered as foolish speculation. It is mainly the rise of evolutionary theory that has caused people to question biblical statements that indicate a young age for the universe and man.

From a biblical perspective there is no need to assume that there are any gaps in the genealogies of Genesis 5 and 11. On the contrary, the scriptures are specific in giving the ages of the fathers when their sons were born, as well as their ages when they themselves died. Furthermore, Jude, writing at the other end of the Bible (Jude 14), confirms that Enoch was the seventh from Adam, so there are no missing parts to the family tree in the first seven generations and as the style of language used remains the same, there is no good reason to suppose that there are any gaps from Enoch to Noah. A similar conclusion can be reached from Genesis 10 and 11 in conjunction with the confirmation of 1 Chronicles 1. God would not leave gaps in His record and at the same time give the impression that this is a continuous, unbroken chronology.

Modern evolutionary theory (Neo-Darwinism) requires the age of the earth to be around 4,600 million years; that of life itself, around 3,000 million years and man around 3 million years. Even allowing for gaps in the genealogical records, scripture indicates human history to be about 10,000 years old at the most, with 6,000 years probably being more accurate, so that a huge discrepancy exists between evolutionary theory and biblical information.

* Archbishop James Ussher was born in Dublin in 1581, died in 1656 and was buried in Westminister Abbey. The English copy of his most famous work, 'The Annals of the World', was published in 1658.

If the first verse of the Bible was re-written from an evolutionary perspective it would have to read something like this -

In the beginning there was nothing, which exploded into something and eventually became everything.

But this hypothesis not only runs counter to scripture but also to the discovered laws of science.

The FIRST LAW OF THERMODYNAMICS states that matter and energy is neither created nor destroyed. Things do not arise out of nothing and there is nothing within the universe that is capable of bringing the universe into being. Even if we begin with something, the problem remains as to where it came from, for matter cannot be eternal.

The SECOND LAW OF THERMODYNAMICS states that all physical systems, when left to themselves, will move in a direction from order to disorder, not from simple to complex. Over a period of time spontaneous processes lead to a decrease in order not an increase, for everything deteriorates or dies.

Order and available energy does not come from an explosion, as is abundantly clear from the results of war. Those who propagate a Big Bang theory from which, they claim, the universe was spontaneously born, are unable to provide a feasible explanation for the source of the initial material. This question remains, for the evolutionist, one of the most awkward and fundamental of all - how did the whole process start? The Bible provides the answer by introducing us on its first page to another realm of existence beyond our own created universe.

Note what scripture links with **'the beginning'**. When Jesus spoke to the Pharisees He said, **'from the beginning of the creation God made them male and female'** and, 'Moses because of the hardness of your hearts suffered you to put away your wives: but from the beginning it was not so' (Mark 10.6, Matthew 19:8).

These scriptures clearly link Adam and Eve with the beginning when God created and made the world, so there is no room here for the long period of time required by evolutionary theory for the arrival of man after evolving for millions of years. For such a scenario there could be no defined 'beginning' of man, for there would be no identifiable point in time when the developing non-man became man. So once again we see that the Bible does not support biological evolution.

The Lord Jesus also said, 'the blood of all the prophets, which was shed from the foundation of the world, may be required of this generation; from the blood of Abel unto the blood of Zacharias' (Luke 11:50/51). In this passage Abel is regarded as having lived around the time when the world was founded, which clearly indicates a short period between Genesis 1.1 and Genesis 4.10. Hence large gaps in the early chapters of Genesis are not indicated by scripture nor are they required.

Satan's activity in the Garden of Eden and in causing the death of Abel (1John 3.12) is also described as taking place at the beginning (John 8.44, 1John 3.8). This cannot mean that the Devil was a sinner from the time he was created, as this would contradict Ezekiel 28.15 and imply that God had created an imperfect being; rather it must refer to Satanic activity in relation to creation at the beginning of time.

This first verse is thus short and simple in its construction but profound in its meaning, revealing the same truth to all mankind, that the whole universe was created by God at the beginning of time.

LESSON 4

THE DEVELOPMENT OF THE EARTH

Genesis 1:2 'And the earth was without form, and void; and darkness was upon the face of the deep. And the Spirit of God moved upon the face of the waters.'

After the initial act of absolute creation, the divine record focuses on the development of the earth rather than the heavens, for this was to be the centre of activity. The word 'was' refers to the earth in the condition described at this particular stage of the creation process, not to its condition as the result of a previous catastrophe. This historical and literal account of creation does not indicate or require any gaps in which other undescribed events are considered to have taken place.

The idea that the earth is billions of years old and that its geological development has been extremely slow and gradual is entrenched in popular opinion. However there is very strong evidence that the history of our planet has been dominated by rapid and catastrophic events over a far shorter, but more dynamic, time period.

In May 1980, Mount St Helens in Washington State, USA erupted and in six minutes flattened 150 square miles of forest. Within a very short time a layer of sediment formed twenty five feet thick and mud flows eroded a canyon up to 140 feet deep, about one-fortieth the size of the Grand Canyon. During the seven years which followed the eruption, 600 feet of strata were formed by the deposits. Volcanoes and other natural disasters like this challenge the conventional thinking as to how the earth works, how it changes and the time scale involved. They provide great support for catastrophism as opposed to uniformitarianism.

Sedimentary rocks account for about 75% of all rock outcrops on the earth's surface. These sedimentary rocks, such as shale, sandstone and conglomerate, are produced as a result of the sediment, carried about in water, settling down as deposits and eventually being cemented together under pressure. One of the most spectacular displays of sedimentary rock formation is found in the Grand Canyon, Arizona, which geologists see as containing a record of earth's history.

In numerous locations across the world there are thousands or even hundreds of thousands of square miles of flat, sedimentary rock strata ranging from a few feet to hundreds of feet thick. There are vast stretches of clean sandstone which would have required currents flowing steadily over great distances to separate the sand from the silt and gravel. Other deposits are composed of large areas of conglomerate (rocks made up from particles of various sizes) which would have required a massive upheaval of surging water to lay down such a deposit across thousands of miles of the earth's surface. Furthermore, in most cases the contact surface between successive, parallel, sedimentary rock layers is smooth and regular which indicates that they were laid down in close succession one on top of another before erosion could take place.

Sedimentary rocks are also of importance in that they contain vast numbers of fossils, which are the preserved remains of living things. For this to happen, rapid burial is essential otherwise the normal processes of decay and destruction will take place very soon after death. In some cases creatures have been buried and fossilized so rapidly that even their delicate soft tissues have been preserved. Large numbers of fossil graveyards have been discovered across the world packed with the remains of many different animals from widely separated regions and different climate zones all thrown together in mass burial grounds. In many instances these fossilized creatures show clear signs of alarm and struggle immediately prior to death. This phenomenon can be likened to the events in Pompeii after the eruption of Mount Vesuvius in AD79 when the pyroclastic flow incinerated the inhabitants instantaneously and the lava entombed them in the positions they were in at the moment of death.

Vast amounts of water and sedimentation on a very large scale are required to bury numerous large creatures in a short time. The slow, gradual processess of evolutionary theory are totally inadequate to account for this widespread phenomenon.

There are many other evident distortions to the earth's crust from ocean beds to mountain ranges which indicate catastrophic activity on a very large scale. There are places where hundreds of thousands of square miles have been engulfed by floods of basaltic lava which must have flowed like rivers in layers thousands of feet thick. Upheavals of this magnitude are not observed today, so that in geological terms, the present is not the key to the past. On the mountains of Ararat, at 14,000 feet, a type of lava is found which is extruded under water and is recognisable by its glass content caused by very rapid cooling. This indicates that these regions were once under water, although mountains may not always have been the height they are today.

From a biblical perspective there is an obvious explanation for all of this. The earth was not only entombed in water at the beginning of creation but 1,656 years later in the days of Noah, unimaginable forces of water were unleashed which completely changed the whole of the earth's surface. When the fountains of the great deep were opened this would probably have included volcanic activity and earth movement on a scale not seen since. The 'windows of heaven' were opened up (Genesis 7.11); this may have allowed for the entrance of meteorites as well as huge volumes of water. These powerful waters surging across the globe would carry huge numbers of living things together with vast amounts of sediment of all sizes which would eventually settle and solidify with the remains of the living things entombed in fossil form.

When we consider these events it becomes apparent that sedimentary rock structures, with their fossilized contents, together with the existence of mass graveyards, are far better explained by the force of vast amounts of water rather than by vast amounts of time. We have all witnessed the devastating effects of localised flooding, earthquakes, hurricanes and volcanic eruption. What then would be the result of the global flood in

Noah's time when the whole earth was involved in massive upheavals and when water covered it for about a year?

Whatever explanations evolutionists put forward it remains an indisputable fact that all such deposits are exactly what we would expect to find after a global flood and they demonstrate that what is observed in the record of the rocks fits the facts of biblical history.

Disastrous natural events today serve as evidence and reminders of the worldwide catastrophe which occurred in Noah's time. There has been an increase in natural disasters leading to loss of life for which man is always ready to provide an explanation, nevertheless these events should serve as warnings that the godless conditions which resulted in the flood have become widespread again and have not gone unnoticed by a righteous God (Acts 17.31; 2 Peter 3.9/10).

Dating techniques such as radiometric testing, have proved to be unreliable although they are still in use. To measure elapsed time accurately we need to be sure of the starting value of the 'clock' being used and that it remains constant and free from all external factors at all times and in all conditions. There is evidence that this is not the case with present methods of dating for there is conflict between different systems and a strong tendency to accept dates which agree with what is expected whilst others are rejected and remain unpublished. Although radio-carbon dating has come up with impressive results when tested against objects whose age was independently known, the method is clearly full of problems. A freshly killed seal dated by the radio-carbon method was shown to have been 'dead' for 1,300 years and the shells of living snails were shown to have 'died' 27,000 years previously. Rock paintings found in the South African bush in 1991 were dated at around 1,200 years old, but later a Capetown resident recognised them as those produced by her at an art class and stolen from her garden. Dating methods that produce errors like these cannot be depended on to give consistent, accurate information.

What evolutionary theory requires is time, lots of it, coupled with random chance events. Some attempt to accommodate evolutionary theory within a biblical framework by putting a large, indefinite time gap between the first two verses of Genesis in order to meet the supposed requirements of long geological ages. Some see in this gap theory (developed around the beginning of the 19th century) the creation and destruction of a previous existence similar to ours which Satan entered after being cast out of heaven and which resulted in complete destruction by God giving rise to the conditions mentioned in verse two. But this creates more problems than it solves, for amongst other questions we have to ask why would God then allow sin to intrude a second time and why is God's mercy being shown to our creation when it was not shown to the first ?

The gap theory when used in an attempt to accommodate evolution would still require a prior cataclysmic destruction of the earth which no evolutionary geologist would accept. It is thus self-defeating in terms of gaining credence within an evolutionary framework. There is no benefit for the Christian in this or any other compromise. Theistic evolution, the belief that God used an evolutionary process to achieve His purpose, represents an unacceptable attempt to reach a compromise between the Bible and the perceived requirements of science.

Satan's fall from his heavenly position, as symbolized in Isaiah 14.12-15 and Ezekiel 28.12-19, clearly must have taken place before Genesis 3.1, and the possibility exists that it does fit between these first two verses, but this would not necessitate a large gap in time.

Life before Adam would mean death before Adam. Scripture teaches that death came as the result of Adam's sin, (Romans 5.12) which clearly indicates that before sin came into the world there was no death. Some would argue that plants died before Adam sinned, but they were produced by God specifically as food for animals and man and cannot be considered as being in the same category as animals and man. Furthermore, it would be contrary to the known character of God for Him to use cruel and inefficient cycles of struggle and death to achieve

His work; an infinite God does not need to experiment using trial and error methods before He gets it right.

The Psalmist writes, 'The works of the LORD are great, studied by all who have pleasure in them. His work is honorable and glorious, And His righteousness endures forever. He has made His wonderful works to be remembered; The LORD is gracious and full of compassion' (Psalm 111.2-4NKJV).

Certain scriptures, often quoted to support the theory of a previous creation, do not in fact lead us to this conclusion. Note the following - 'I beheld the earth, and, lo, it was without form, and void; (as used in Genesis 1.2, unformed and unfilled) and the heavens, and they had no light' (Jeremiah 4:23).

'Behold, the LORD maketh the earth empty, and maketh it waste, and turneth it upside down, and scattereth abroad the inhabitants thereof. .... The land shall be utterly emptied, and utterly spoiled: for the LORD hath spoken this word' (Isaiah 24.1 - 3).

In context, these verses do not speak of God's work in creation but describe His view of the nation and land of Israel after His declared intention to make both desolate because of continual sin. These verses began to be fulfilled in 606 B.C. when Nebuchadnezzar came against Jerusalem (2 Kings 24).

Consider also this verse - 'For thus saith the LORD that created (to bring into existence that which had not existed before) the heavens; God himself that formed (to squeeze into shape as a potter) the earth and made it; (from existing materials) he hath established it, (prepared, set up, made ready, arranged in order) he created it not in vain, (to be empty, to lie waste) he formed it to be inhabited: (to be a dwelling place to be lived in) I am the LORD; and there is none else' (Isaiah 45:18).

Rather than supporting the theory of a prior creation, this verse actually does the opposite, for it shows how God's intended purposes were worked out in an orderly way. The four words (created, formed, made, established) are significant for they confirm that Genesis 1 presents us with a progressive, unbroken sequence of events. Creation is again described as a process in which God did not stop, nor was He interrupted, at any stage, leaving his work incomplete. God always finishes what He sets out to do. He created the earth in order for it to be inhabited and that is exactly what had happened by the end of the creation week.

So at this early stage the earth was unstructured, empty, dark and lifeless; a work God had begun but had not yet completed. It was covered by water so that no land had emerged, and the water was covered with darkness. Some would say that God does not produce darkness but in Isaiah God says, 'I form (as a potter) the light, and create (as Genesis 1.1) darkness' (Isaiah 45.7). Light is not described as being created for it has always existed as an essential part of the character of God, (1Timothy 6.16; 1John 1.5; ;Revelation 21.23). Darkness here does not necessarily indicate the presence of evil but rather the incompleteness of the creation process.

The Spirit of God was hovering over the water, moving to and fro, up and down, like a bird over its nest, ready to continue the great purposes of God in relation to earth and to man. He is the great Energiser who sets things in motion, as He did with the establishment of the church (Acts 2.2-4), and will yet do in the re-gathering of Israel, (Ezekiel 37.1-10) The Greek translation of the Old Testament, known as the Septuagint (LXX), uses a word for ' moved' which is also found in 2 Peter 1.21, meaning ' carried along'. There it describes how the writers of the Old Testament were directed by the Spirit in what they wrote. The Holy Spirit is thus the power behind the formation of God's world and the formation of God's Word. His work is essential before anything can be achieved for God.

LESSON 5

Day 1 - DARKNESS AND LIGHT

Genesis 1:3-5 'And God said, Let there be light: and there was light. 4 And God saw the light, that it was good: and God divided the light from the darkness. 5 And God called the light Day, and the darkness he called Night. And the evening and the morning were the first day.'

Each of the creation days begins with God speaking (see verses 6, 9, 14, 20, 24) and it seems reasonable, therefore, to believe that the first day also begins in this way with this verse. Light, an essential part of a day, is produced at this stage.

During the first three days God deals with the unformed earth providing it with light, air, water and land. During the second three days God deals with the unfilled earth producing lights, birds, sea creatures, animals and man.

Note the correspondence -

Forming	Filling
Day 1 - light	Day 4 - light sources
Day 2 - water and air	Day 5 - water and air animals
Day 3 - land	Day 6 - land animals

God works methodically and in the unfolding days of creation He establishes principles which can be traced throughout the whole of scripture. Some of these will be referred to later in this course.

Here, in the phrase 'God said' is the first of ten commandments all of which were fulfilled, in contrast to another more well known set of ten commandments in Exodus 20, all of which have been broken by man. God's spoken word brought an instantaneous and exact response. There is no time gap between the command and the commencement of its fulfilment.

'By the word of the LORD the heavens were made, And all the host of them by the breath of His mouth. He gathers the waters of the sea together as a heap; He lays up the deep in storehouses. Let all the earth fear the LORD; Let all the inhabitants of the world stand in awe of Him. For He spoke, and it was done; He commanded, and it stood fast' (Psalms 33.6 - 9 NKJV).

Similarly in the New Testament, when the Lord Jesus spoke there was an instant response. To the stormy wind and waves He said, 'peace be still. And the wind ceased, and there was a great calm.' (Mark 4.39); to Lazarus He said, 'come forth. And he that was dead came forth' (John 11.43), and to the leper Jesus said, 'be thou clean, and immediately his leprosy was cleansed' (Matthew 8.3). The phrase which follows ('let there be') indicates that no event happened of itself but only as a result of, and on the authority of, the spoken word of God.

God is light (1 John 1.5) and He dwells in light (1 Timothy 6.16). It is not surprising, therefore, to see that God produced light in the universe before He made the sun which was to control the light from day four. The New Testament confirms that God, 'commanded the light to shine out of darkness' (2 Corinthians 4.6) for the same God has shed light into our darkened hearts. The Christian can bear personal testimony to this aspect of the creation account because he/she is able to say, 'it has happened to me.'

The phrase 'and God saw', occurs seven times in this passage and it shows that God examined what He had done and found that it was exactly as He intended. He took pleasure in what He did, which would hardly be true if millions of years of cruel evolution had taken place.

God personally names five things which needed to be defined from the start. Here it is Day and Night; later He names Heaven, Earth, and Seas. The distinction between light and darkness (daylight and night-time) indicates the structure and completion of the first day.

Each successive day was marked by an evening and a morning. Between each evening and morning there was a period of darkness and between each morning and evening there was a period of light. Together these constituted a normal twenty-four hour day, as indeed they still do.

From Day 4 onwards the onset of the evening and the morning has been marked by sunset and sunrise respectively. By referring to the evenings first, the pattern of Day 1 has been continued for on this first day God brought light out of the darkness.

Some would rightly point out that 'day' can mean a longer period of time, as in Genesis 2.4 or in the phrase 'the day of the Lord'. However, in the Old Testament, every time the Hebrew word for day (yom) is qualified by a number it means a day of twenty four hours. If God had wanted to convey the idea that the days of creation were long periods of time He could simply have used another more suitable word, but instead He employed the word commonly used for a solar day for that is exactly the meaning God intended to convey.

Could all these events happen in six days ? When an all-intelligent, all-powerful God is at work it could have been achieved in six seconds ! Jeremiah says, 'He has made the earth by His power, He has established the world by His wisdom, And has stretched out the heavens at His discretion' (Jeremiah 10.12NKJV; see also Proverbs 3.19, Isaiah 40.26) Some would maintain that the day here is symbolic, but a word cannot be symbolic the first time it is used, it has to be literal first in order to establish its primary meaning.

Let us suppose that this word 'day' means 1000 years, which some conclude from 2 Peter 3.8 ('one day is with the Lord as a thousand years, and a thousand years as one day'); then Adam, who was created

In the Beginning   **EXAM 1**

Name ....

Address ....

....

Course Tutor .... Mark ....

Lesson 1 & 2

1.   Why is neither Evolution nor Creation capable of scientific
      investigation?

....

....

....

....

....

2.   What are the essential differences between an evolutionary
      and biblical approach to origins?

....

....

....

....

....

3.   In what two ways can a Christian answer the claims of evolution?

....

....

....

....

....

....

....

4.　Explain in your own words the meanings of Hebrews 11 verses 3 and 6.

....
....
....
....
....
....

5.　Why is Genesis so important as a foundation?

....
....
....
....
....
....

6.　How does the New Testament confirm the accuracy of the book of Genesis?

....
....
....
....
....

7.　What is the evidence for Genesis 1: 1-2:3 being a continuous account?

....
....
....
....
....

PLEASE enclose a **SUITABLE** stamped addressed envelope for the return of your corrected exam.
POST TO: EMMAUS BIBLE SCHOOL U.K., Carlett Boulevard, Eastham, Wirral, England CH62 8BZ. FOR MARKING.
GROUP STUDY MEMBERS, hand to your group leader.

In the Beginning   **EXAM 2**

Name ....

Address ....

....

Course Tutor .... Mark ....

Lesson 3 & 4

1. What does scripture teach about the work of the Son of God
    in creation?

    ....
    ....
    ....
    ....
    ....

2. What are we to understand about time, energy, space and
    matter?

    ....
    ....
    ....
    ....
    ....

3. What light does Jude throw on the genealogies of Genesis?

    ....
    ....
    ....
    ....
    ....
    ....
    ....

4. What can we learn from scriptures which speak about 'the beginning'?

....

....

....

....

....

5. How could a global flood account for the present structure of the earth's surface?

....

....

....

....

....

6. What are some of the problems involved in trying to fit evolutionary theory into the Biblical account of creation?

....

....

....

....

....

7. In what way does Isaiah 45:18 explain God's work as a process?

....

....

....

....

....

PLEASE enclose a **SUITABLE** stamped addressed envelope for the return of your corrected exam.
POST TO: EMMAUS BIBLE SCHOOL U.K., Carlett Boulevard, Eastham, Wirral, England CH62 8BZ. FOR MARKING.
GROUP STUDY MEMBERS, hand to your group leader.

Name ....

Address ....

....

Course Tutor .... Mark ....

Lesson 5 & 6

1. What parallels can be seen between the first three days and the second three days of creation?

....
....
....
....
....

2. Which New Testament incidents support the view that God's spoken word brought an instantaneous response?

....
....
....
....
....

3. Briefly explain the five things that God named.

....
....
....
....
....
....
....

4.   What does Exodus confirm about the creation process?

....
....
....
....
....

5.   How could the two water layers be responsible for the flood in Noah's day?

....
....
....
....
....

6.   What are the three 'heavens' mentioned in the Bible?

....
....
....
....
....

7.   Summarise the first two days of creation.

....
....
....
....
....
....
....

PLEASE enclose a **SUITABLE** stamped addressed envelope for the return of your corrected exam.
POST TO: EMMAUS BIBLE SCHOOL U.K., Carlett Boulevard, Eastham, Wirral, England CH62 8BZ. FOR MARKING.
GROUP STUDY MEMBERS, hand to your group leader.

E 6

Name ....

Address ....

....

Course Tutor .... Mark ....

Lessons 7 & 8

1. Give a possible explanation of the earth being divided in
    the days of Peleg.

    ....

    ....

    ....

    ....

    ....

2. Explain the importance of the phrase 'after his/its kind'?

    ....

    ....

    ....

    ....

    ....

3. What are the main roles of the sun, moon and stars?

    ....

    ....

    ....

    ....

    ....

    ....

    ....

4. What can the miracles in the gospels tell us about the creation process?

....
....
....
....
....

5. What is the significance of the phrase 'and it was so'?

....
....
....
....
....

6. Why do many people not believe in the existence of God?

....
....
....
....
....

7. Why is the earth of far greater importance than any other planet?

....
....
....
....
....

PLEASE enclose a **SUITABLE** stamped addressed envelope for the return of your corrected exam.
POST TO: EMMAUS BIBLE SCHOOL U.K., Carlett Boulevard, Eastham, Wirral, England CH62 8BZ. FOR MARKING.
GROUP STUDY MEMBERS, hand to your group leader.

Name ....

Address ....

....

Course Tutor .... Mark ....

Lesson 9 & 10

1. What is the biblical evidence for dinosaurs and their existence at the same time as man?

....

....

....

....

....

2. What are the implications of God describing His work as 'good'.

....

....

....

....

....

3. Give some examples of microevolution and its limitations.

....

....

....

....

....

....

....

4. Explain the significance of the evolutionary 'tree' and the biblical 'forest'.

....

....

....

....

....

5. Explain man's uniqueness in possessing body, soul and spirit.

....

....

....

....

....

6. What scriptures teach us that man is far superior to the animals?

....

....

....

....

....

7. Explain the three uses of the word 'created' in Genesis 1.

....

....

....

....

....

....

PLEASE enclose a **SUITABLE** stamped addressed envelope for the return of your corrected exam.
POST TO: EMMAUS BIBLE SCHOOL U.K., Carlett Boulevard, Eastham, Wirral, England CH62 8BZ. FOR MARKING.
GROUP STUDY MEMBERS, hand to your group leader.

Name ....

Address ....

....

Course Tutor .... Mark ....

Lesson 11 & 12

1.   What is the link between Genesis 1.1 and 2.1?
....
....
....
....
....

2.   Why did God rest on the seventh day?
....
....
....
....
....

3.   What does Exodus tell us about the Sabbath day?
....
....
....
....
....
....
....

4. How were records of the creation and the flood spread after Babel?

....
....
....
....
....

5. What are some of the logical implications of evolutionary theory?

....
....
....
....
....

6. Outline some practical applications from the events of the first three days.

....
....
....
....
....

7. Outline some practical applications from the events of days 4 to 7.

....
....
....
....
....

PLEASE enclose a **SUITABLE** stamped addressed envelope for the return of your corrected exam.
POST TO: EMMAUS BIBLE SCHOOL U.K., Carlett Boulevard, Eastham, Wirral, England CH62 8BZ. FOR MARKING.
GROUP STUDY MEMBERS, hand to your group leader.

E 12

on day six, would be 1000 years of age on day seven. However, Adam's third son, Seth, was born when Adam was 130 (Genesis 5.3) and Adam died at the age of 930 (Genesis 5.5), so that the word 'day' , in the creation account, cannot mean 1000 years or anything near it. (Peter is showing that the passage of time, so important to men, does not affect the accomplishment of the promises of God).

When reading our bibles it should be borne in mind that God has not presented us with a book of puzzles for us to solve as best we can. We are not faced with a whole set of problems in which certain answers cannot be right because they are too obvious. The Bible has been written to clarify and inform not to mystify and mislead. God desires to make His mind known to man and we should therefore accept plain statements of scripture at face value, with their ordinary literal meaning, unless there are clear reasons for doing otherwise. The comparing of scripture with scripture is essential in this process.

An insistence on long periods of time can simply be an attempt to accommodate evolution within a Genesis time-frame and so to add 'respectability' to our faith. In the creation account, it was clearly the writer's intention to convey a literal six-day creation and this interpretation is confirmed by other scriptures.

'For in six days the LORD made heaven and earth, the sea, and all that in them is, and rested the seventh day: wherefore the LORD blessed the sabbath day, and hallowed it' (Exodus 20:11).

'It is a sign between me and the children of Israel for ever: for in six days the LORD made heaven and earth, and on the seventh day he rested, and was refreshed' (Exodus 31.17).

Note in these verses that the seventh day is the same as the sabbath day, which, from its numerous uses in scripture, is clearly a day of normal length. If therefore the seventh day is of standard duration so are also the preceding six days.

The sabbath day is our Saturday, the last day of the week, so the first day of creation week was a Sunday - a day also of significance in other scriptures (Mark 16.1,2,9; Acts 20.7). In this first seven-day period God was establishing an order for man to follow; a pattern for life, a weekly cycle leading up to rest.

LESSON 6

Day 2 - THE DIVIDING OF THE WATERS

Genesis 1:6-8 'And God said, Let there be a firmament in the midst of the waters, and let it divide the waters from the waters. 7. And God made the firmament, and divided the waters which were under the firmament from the waters which were above the firmament: and it was so. 8. And God called the firmament Heaven. And the evening and the morning were the second day.'

On this second day, the water, which completely covered the earth, was divided through the middle by an expanse or space. As this non-water layer expanded it raised the upper layer of water high above the earth leaving the lower layer on the earth. We do not know what form this upper layer of water took; but it would most likely have been a canopy of water vapour, which unlike clouds, would be invisible and transparent so that light could shine through onto the earth.

The effect of such a canopy would be that a uniformly, warm temperature would be maintained all over the world with the absence of winds and storms. It would also produce lush vegetation with no areas of barrenness and any harmful rays from outer space would be filtered out.

The two water layers were on either side of an expanse which God called 'heaven', and which we know as the sky, the atmosphere above us. The water remains on earth today but no longer above the earth except in cloud form. One explanation for this is that when 'the windows of heaven were opened' in Noah's time, the huge water vapour canopy condensed and poured onto the earth producing the world-wide flood recorded in Genesis chapter seven. Massive underground caverns, the 'foundations of the great deep' also released their contents onto the earth's surface (Genesis 7.11,8.2).

The Bible speaks of the water cycle in which clouds condense into rain, which falls on the ground and in the waters and eventually returns back to the clouds through the process of evaporation. Solomon wrote, 'All the rivers run into the sea; yet the sea is not full; unto the place from whence the rivers come, thither they return again' (Ecclesiastes 1.7). Jeremiah also states, 'When he uttereth his voice, there is a multitude of waters in the heavens, and he causeth the vapours to ascend from the ends of the earth; he maketh lightnings with rain, and bringeth forth the wind out of his treasures' (Jeremiah 10.13).

The water cycle would not be operative until after the flood for it seems that clouds were not formed and therefore there was no rain until the flood. Prior to this a vapour came up from the ground to water the earth. (Genesis 2.5/6)

The precision and accuracy of God's work is recorded by Isaiah when he asks, 'Who hath measured the waters in the hollow of his hand, and meted out heaven with the span, and comprehended the dust of the earth in a measure, and weighed the mountains in scales, and the hills in a balance?' (Isaiah 40.12)

The Bible speaks of three heavens - the atmospheric heaven or sky; the stellar heaven, the place of the planets and stars, and thirdly the abode of God, to which Paul was taken when 'caught up to the third heaven.' (2 Corinthians 12.2), where Christ now is (Hebrews 9.24) and where all Christians will soon be (2 Corinthians 5.1).

So the first two days involved the division of the darkness and the deep, and the provision of water, light and air in anticipation of further developments. God systematically prepared an environment which was entirely suited for the establishment and maintenance of life.

LESSON 7

Day 3 - THE DRY LAND

Genesis 1:9-13 'And God said, Let the waters under the heaven be gathered together unto one place, and let the dry land appear: and it was so. 10. And God called the dry land Earth; and the gathering together of the waters called he Seas: and God saw that it was good. 11 And God said, Let the earth bring forth grass, the herb yielding seed, and the fruit tree yielding fruit after his kind, whose seed is in itself, upon the earth: and it was so. 12 And the earth brought forth grass, and herb yielding seed after his kind, and the tree yielding fruit, whose seed was in itself, after his kind: and God saw that it was good. 13 And the evening and the morning were the third day.'

The water which still covered the earth like a shoreless ocean was brought together into one place and called 'Seas'. The dry land emerged (probably also one land mass) and was called 'Earth'. This probably involved the lowering of the ocean floor and the raising of the land mass with much water being stored in huge reservoirs under the earth. The New Testament speaks of, 'the earth standing out of water and in water,' (2 Peter 3.5/6) and this water flooded the earth again in Noah's day in an act of divine judgement. Peter reminds us that the same authoritative word of God has reserved the present heavens and earth for future judgement.

The earth probably remained as one land mass until the flood, after which it began to break up with the parts moving away from each other. The continents, as seen today, do not fit together at sea level, but at a depth of about 900 metres the contours of the exposed continental shelves can be seen to fit back together into their original places quite well. For example, the east coast of South America fits nicely into the west coast of Africa. Although geologists recognise the existence, at

41

one time, of a single land mass (Pangaea - "all land") the time scale and explanations usually offered depend on an evolutionary model.

The break up of the original land mass would require massive forces such as those generated by the flood and its subsequent effects. Maybe this began to happen in the days of Peleg, for 'in his days was the earth divided' (Genesis 10.25). Peleg was born 101 years after the flood and died at the age of 239 years (Genesis 11.16-19). The purpose, perhaps, of the division of the land mass was to ensure that the nations remained dispersed throughout the earth as God intended and not as man intended at Babel (Genesis 11.4). It is interesting to note that from the birth of Peleg there was a substantial shortening of the lifespan.

The sea and the land is God's work and God's property. 'The sea is his, and he made it: and his hands formed the dry land (Psalm 95.5). God has, 'placed the sand for the bound of the sea by a perpetual decree, that it cannot pass it: and though the waves thereof toss themselves, yet can they not prevail; though they roar, yet can they not pass over it?' (Jeremiah 5.22).

God speaks for the fourth time and this results in the first self-propagating vegetation. He furnishes the earth by spreading a carpet of green across the ground in the form of grass, herbs and trees, intended as a food source for living creatures and man. It seems here that in the bringing forth of this first vegetation, what now takes days, months or years to fully develop took place instantaneously or within a day, so that it had the appearance of age. God intended to finish His work in six days not to extend it over a long period of time. This is an important factor which will be referred to again later.

The phrase 'after his kind' occurs ten times in the creation account and it shows how every living organism has a built-in ability to reproduce itself. The information and mechanism required to produce another of the same kind lies within each living thing. There is no suggestion, no provision, and no necessity for one form of life to evolve into another entirely different form (macroevolution), for God produced a huge variety at the beginning.

42

The genetical information in each cell was predetermined by God, the Master Designer who possesses infinite intelligence. We do not know exactly what 'kind' means, but it clearly indicates a closed, identifiable group designed to reproduce within itself but not outside of itself. God made a huge range of 'kinds', each of which were capable of reproducing new varieties within the limitations of their own group (microevolution). For an entirely new species to arise from an existing one (macroevolution), new genetic information would be required, not just a re-arrangement of what already exists.

These first life forms were certainly not simple as evolutionary theory has taught. Cells, the building blocks of life, are highly specialised units whether found in micro-organisms or humans. The DNA in each cell contains a huge library of coded information which is stored as the genetic blueprint for passing on to the next generation. The DNA from the male and female parents is "read" like an instruction manual in the construction of the new organism.

Scientists have been unable to create life; even if they did, it would prove that intelligence is needed to produce living things. Life is complex beyond our understanding, yet we are expected to believe that it not only arose of itself but has developed such complexity by natural means. The wonderful design inherent in living things clearly indicates the work of an intelligent, purposeful Designer.

Plant life exists because of the thin layer of soil on the earth's outer layer which consists mainly of minerals (45%), water (25%) and air (25%). The earth has been built by God with all the materials necessary for the maintenance of life.

After the first three days the FORMING process was complete; the earth with its water, light, air, land and food supply was ready for its inhabitants. The next three days describe the FILLING and functioning of the earth.

LESSON 8

Day 4 - LIGHTS IN THE HEAVENS

Genesis 1:14-19 'And God said, Let there be lights in the firmament of the heaven to divide the day from the night; and let them be for signs, and for seasons, and for days, and years: 15 And let them be for lights in the firmament of the heaven to give light upon the earth: and it was so. 16 And God made two great lights; the greater light to rule the day, and the lesser light to rule the night: he made the stars also. 17 And God set them in the firmament of the heaven to give light upon the earth, 18 And to rule over the day and over the night, and to divide the light from the darkness: and God saw that it was good. 19 And the evening and the morning were the fourth day.'

In this fifth commandment God establishes the vast array of heavenly bodies in their places with particular reference to the sun and the moon in relation to earth. It has to be assumed that the sun's family of planets, the solar system, is also included, although nothing specific is said about them here. Unlike earth the planets can be seen as remaining waste and empty, unsuitable for habitation, as the earth was at one stage. God did not develop them further to be places that would sustain life.

The whole of scripture bears testimony to the uniqueness of earth as the centre of life, containing everything necessary for the sustaining of living things. The stability and equilibrium of earth's systems are remarkably sensitive to precise values - for us to be here, things must be exactly as they are. However, the most significant biblical evidence for the uniqueness of earth is the wonderful fact that the Son of God, the Creator Himself, came here many centuries ago (1John 4.14) and this is the place to which He will return very soon to claim His own people (1 Thessalonians 4.16/17) and to set up His glorious kingdom

(Luke 1.33). Again it has to be stated, no theories of men could ever lead to such amazing truths.

God placed the sun and the moon in the heavens to -
1. Direct light onto the earth. 2. Divide time into days and years.
3. Determine the seasons.   4. Declare the presence & power of God.

Jeremiah refers to God as the one who, 'gives the sun for a light by day, The ordinances of the moon and the stars for a light by night, Who disturbs the sea, and its waves roar. The LORD of hosts is His name' (Jeremiah 31.35NKJV)

These heavenly bodies have been and will yet be signs to man. A star (perhaps one of a special nature) led the wise men to Christ (Matthew 2.2) and in the near future the sun and the moon and the stars will give clear signs of the end of the age (Luke 21.25/26). But again man has misread God's revelation and has corrupted God's heavenly display of His glory, worshipping the things created rather than the Creator (Romans 1.25); preferring to follow a system of pagan astrology instead of the living God (Acts 7.42, 14.12-15). The nation of Israel was warned against this (Deuteronomy 4.19).

The vastness of space is a truly wonderful spectacle reflecting the greatness of God. The stars cannot be numbered by man but God knows every one by name (Psalm 147.4). God says, 'Lift up your eyes on high, and behold who hath created these things, that bringeth out their host by number: he calleth them all by names by the greatness of his might, for that he is strong in power; not one faileth' (Isaiah 40.26). Each star is different in its splendour, such is the variety of God's handiwork (1Corinthians 15.41). Distances across space are enormous; the nearest star, Proxima Centauri, is about 26 million, million miles away and it would take its light more than four years to reach earth travelling at 186,300 miles per second.

We have already noted that earth's first vegetation grew to full size in less than a day and this same principle probably applies here. God speeded up the first effects of the light from the stars so that it reached earth either instantaneously or within a day. He did not design lengthy processes that delayed the implementation of His main objective - the creation of man. This does not raise a problem, for an omnipotent God can do anything; He does not need to follow the rules of science from a textbook for He devised them in the first place and can work outside of them at any time He chooses. The gospels record about thirty-five specific miracles performed by the Lord Jesus, every one of which were contrary to the laws of nature. This is God's prerogative.

Seasons refer to appointed durations of time, but perhaps not to seasons functioning as we know them until after the flood (Genesis 8.22). A day, as we have have already noted, is of twenty-four hours duration and consists of one revolution of the earth on its axis. A year is reckoned as one revolution of the earth around the sun.

God had already set day and night in motion, now He sets these lights to take control of what had already been established. The solar system, revolving against a background of stars, is, in very simple terms, like the fingers of a clock rotating against its face which man is able to read and so is able to measure the passing of time and to determine geographical position and direction.

The phrase 'and it was so' occurs six times in this account and it indicates that there was no resistance to what God said; His command was carried out without delay and in exactly the way He intended.

According to evolutionary theory, time is needed to account for the complexity and variety of living forms seen today. Vast amounts of time are injected and intelligence is extracted, leaving the evolutionary process the result of numerous chance, random events over millions of years. However, the idea of randomness is subject to the laws of mathematical probability which when applied to evolutionary theory demonstrate that the chances of huge, ordered sequences of specific, beneficial events taking place to be so remote as to be equated with the impossible - and the impossible does not become probable by involving incomprehensibly long ages; the mathematical evidence is to the contrary.

In the search for intelligent life elsewhere in the universe, radio telescopes look for regular, non-random, sequences of signals coming in from outer space that show pattern and design as indicating the existence of other beings. Yet the abundance of evidence for design right here on earth is not regarded by many as clear proof of an intelligent Designer.

Accepting the concept of a God who is actively involved in the creation and maintenance of the universe is regarded by many as unscientific and an obstacle to reaching a well-reasoned conclusion. To believe in God is to acknowledge that He is in full control, whereas man is driven on by his own desire to conquer and control. The foundation of man's thinking is antagonistic to God for the human mind in its natural state is opposed to Him. Romans 1.28 tells us that men, 'did not like to retain God in their knowledge.' This is why Christians cannot rely on the thinking and conclusions of men who do not know God, especially when it comes to spiritual matters (Romans 8.7; 1 Corinthians 2.14). Those who have come to know God through acceptance by faith of His Son, have intelligence and understanding well beyond those who do not know Him.

We are part of a galaxy known as the Milky Way, which is itself part of a group of galaxies with more star clusters penetrating deep into space. In view of the enormity of space we may well ask why the earth is so special. Stars are enormous gaseous bodies which are comparatively simple in structure. The Earth, which is not a by-product of a star or other heavenly body for it was created first, is far more complex with its surface layer of soil, its water supply and its surrounding atmosphere which support life. Much more information was needed to make the earth than the stars or planets for it is only here that God has placed such an enormous variety of life with many highly organised structures, especially the human brain - three pounds of the most complex and highly ordered material in the universe. The human body, the Psalmist reminds us, is 'fearfully and wonderfully made' (Psalm 139.14).

Earth is not only the centre of complexity but also the centre of activity. God's attention is focused here, for this little planet of ours is central to the great purposes of God. The Son of God has been here; He was born here when He 'became flesh' (John1.14); He lived here; He died here and He is soon to return here. The revelation of truth that the scriptures bring to us is vastly superior to anything that we could learn through man-made theories. We view everything from a far higher perspective when we recognise the authority of scripture.

Christians can admire and enjoy the wonders of the created world and then by faith look beyond to the uncreated world and so begin to grasp something of the mightiness and exceeding greatness of our God.

LESSON 9

Day 5 - LIFE IN THE SEA AND AIR

Genesis 1:20-23 'And God said, Let the waters bring forth abundantly the moving creature that hath life, and fowl that may fly above the earth in the open firmament of heaven. 21 And God created great whales, and every living creature that moveth, which the waters brought forth abundantly, after their kind, and every winged fowl after his kind: and God saw that it was good. 22 And God blessed them, saying, Be fruitful, and multiply, and fill the waters in the seas, and let fowl multiply in the earth. 23 And the evening and the morning were the fifth day.'

God now populates the earth's environments in the order in which they were produced - water, air then land. He again turns His attention to the waters for the previously barren seas now swarm with life as God designs and creates living creatures suited to this environment. He then produces flying creatures designed and made for movement in the air. God populates the water and the air with a vast variety of living things all produced on the same day and all programmed to reproduce within built-in limits, resulting eventually in an even greater variety, each capable of adapting to its own environment.

The word translated 'great whales' implies large creatures or monsters. There are two other words used in the Old Testament, 'leviathan' and 'behemoth'. whose descriptions sound very much like what we now call dinosaurs; a word coined in 1841 by Richard Owen meaning 'terrible lizard'.

God describes these creatures to Job; 'Out of his mouth go burning lamps, and sparks of fire leap out. Out of his nostrils goeth smoke, as out of a seething pot or caldron. His breath kindleth coals, and a flame goeth out of his mouth' (Job 41.19 - 21).

49

'Look now at the behemoth, which I made along with you; He eats grass like an ox. See now, his strength is in his hips, And his power is in his stomach muscles. He moves his tail like a cedar; The sinews of his thighs are tightly knit. His bones are like beams of bronze, His ribs like bars of iron.' (Job 40.15 - 18 NKJV).

There are no known animals today that answer to these descriptions, but there is abundant evidence of their existence in the fossil records for hundreds of dinosaur skeletons have been found, many of them complete. Evolutionists believe that dinosaurs died out 60-70 million years ago and that man came about 3 million years ago, yet Job, who probably lived around the time of Abraham, was familiar with huge creatures which seem to answer to the description of dinosaurs.

Historical literature from various countries speaks of large, fire breathing animals and there is usually at least an element of truth in the origin of these stories. Certainly the translators of the Authorised Version of the Bible (1611) had no problem in using the word 'dragon', (eg Isaiah 27.1, Jeremiah 51.34).

If life was millions of years old the earth would be crammed with the remains of vast numbers of creatures from all of the numerous intermediary stages of development. We would not need to search for 'missing links' but would find them readily on every hand and from every stage of the vast evolutionary process. However, the most significant thing about ' missing links ' is that they are missing!

The evolutionary scenario of the spontaneous eruption of something out of nothing and then of everything else out of that something is a philosophical proposition not a scientific fact. At its base lies the desire of many to prove that belief in the existence of God is unnecessary.

So the planet began to teem with an abundance of living things in the sea and air. God clearly found great joy and pleasure in such activity. (Read Job 38) Living things were to reproduce and become numerous (Psalm 104.24/25), for it was God's clear intention to fill the whole earth with life.

Here again as with plant life, each living kind has its own, distinctive, built-in, genetic code. Although 'kind' refers to recognisable groups or genetic banks, a great variety has developed, as God intended, within these groups. This pool of genetic information allows for and ensures, wide diversification and adaptation within determined limits.

God's declaration that His work was good could not be said if evolution had occurred, but there is no continual process of struggle, death and decay in the Genesis record, for God would find no pleasure whatsoever in such cruel and destructive methods - the survival of the fittest. Evolution describes an ugly process whereas God, as a reflection of His own character, does wonderful things, as indisputably demonstrated when He sent His Son to be the Saviour of the world. Theories of evolution totally ignore the presence, the power and the purposes of God in creation.

The teaching of evolutionary theory is that microevolution extends into macroevolution in which complex organisms keep on changing in very, very small steps. Some believe these steps to be larger and less frequent. However, each of these steps would have to result in a fully functioning, living system which gives survival advantage over the original system. In complex living organisms each part is inextricably interrelated to other parts so that change in one part only is highly unlikely to produce a more efficient organism - it is far more likely to produce one that does not function at all. Evolution proposes that finely balanced and highly complex biological systems can change from one thing to another without passing through non-functional intermediates, but this would require many simultaneous changes at cellular level to produce an advantageous result. Consider, for example, the enormous complexities of the eye and the great number of processes that would have to be co-ordinated in order to develop together; and all as a result of chance, random changes.

To be functional, all organs must be complete. An incomplete, non-functioning part does not give an organism any advantage. There are also numerous examples of specialization within living things that could not have developed gradually but needed to be fully formed and operational from the start to ensure the organisms survival. The evidence indicates that living things are functioning at their optimum in relation to their own structure and to the environment in which they live.

It remains an irrefutable fact that the earth is finely tuned for life. The unanimous testimony of everything that exists points again and again to this unavoidable conclusion - we are meant to be here. God has left His fingerprints all over His wonderful creation. (Psalm 8.3/4) If, in spite of the abundance of evidence, we miss God, we miss everything of lasting value.

LESSON 10

Day 6 - LAND ANIMALS AND MAN

Genesis 1:24-31 'And God said, Let the earth bring forth the living creature after his kind, cattle, and creeping thing, and beast of the earth after his kind: and it was so. 25 And God made the beast of the earth after his kind, and cattle after their kind, and every thing that creepeth upon the earth after his kind: and God saw that it was good. And God said, Let us make man in our image, after our likeness: and let them have dominion over the fish of the sea, and over the fowl of the air, and over the cattle, and over all the earth, and over every creeping thing that creepeth upon the earth. 27 So God created man in his own image, in the image of God created he him; male and female created he them. 28 And God blessed them, and God said unto them, Be fruitful, and multiply, and replenish (fill) the earth, and subdue it: and have dominion over the fish of the sea, and over the fowl of the air, and over every living thing that moveth upon the earth. 29 And God said, Behold, I have given you every herb bearing seed, which is upon the face of all the earth, and every tree, in the which is the fruit of a tree yielding seed; to you it shall be for meat. 30 And to every beast of the earth, and to every fowl of the air, and to every thing that creepeth upon the earth, wherein there is life, I have given every green herb for meat: and it was so. 31 And God saw every thing that he had made, and, behold, it was very good. And the evening and the morning were the sixth day.'

God's last day of work involved the production of land creatures, described as cattle, creeping things and beasts. It is difficult to identify these three types of animal groupings, but clearly they could be distinguished for they are often mentioned in scripture, eg Genesis 7.14, 8.17, Psalm 148.10.

The first diagram below shows the evolutionary idea of all things developing from a single cell, with the dotted lines representing hypothetical links to all other living things. The second diagram shows the biblical idea of original, distinctive kinds subsequently developing within limits. Neo-Dawinism regards mammals, for example, as having descended from a single, unidentified, land mammal. Yet for this to have happened huge numbers of intermediate species in direct line of transition must have existed, but the fossil record fails to reveal even one. Of the thousands upon thousands of intermediates that should be readily found, evolutionists are only able to point to a mere handful of questionable examples. Rather than showing the occurrence of macroevolution from one species to another, the fossil record confirms that things have remained within the 'kinds' as God created them.

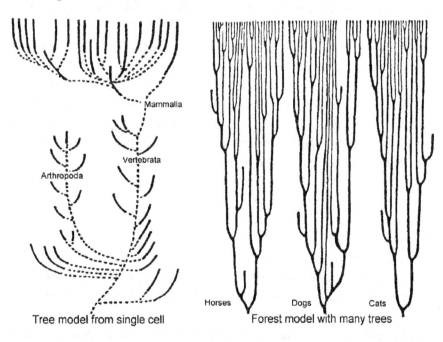

Tree model from single cell   Forest model with many trees

Microevolution has clearly taken place as evidenced, for example, in the numerous varieties of dog which have developed from the original dog kind as a result of its built-in potential for genetic variability. Dogs, as we know them, can interbreed with wolves, coyotes, jackals and foxes to give fertile offspring. It is also clear that many animals cannot interbreed and this is evidence of the limitations God built-in to preserve the distinctiveness of each kind. Experiments in selective breeding have shown that many animals and plants are capable of a considerable amount of change, but end-points are eventually reached beyond which it is not possible to go.

Here in this section we read of dialogue within the Godhead ('let us') which shows that God is plural in His being as already indicated in verse one where a plural word for ' God ' is used. This truth of God being Father, Son and Spirit, is repeated on numerous occasions in other scriptures. (eg Matthew 3.16/17, 28.19, Ephesians 2.18, 1John 5.7) Here we learn of converse within the Godhead as to the creation of man, which shows that God was about to create something special.

The root of the word 'image' means to shade, so that as a shadow represents its substance, so man represents God on earth. There is also a likeness or resemblance between God and man. Seth had a physical resemblance to Adam, (Genesis 5.3) but here man's similarity to God is in the spiritual dimension, for we too are eternal beings like God Himself. Man also is a trinity of being in himself for he consists of body, soul and spirit (1Thessalonians 5.23).

> The **body** makes us world conscious and enables us to interact with our environment through our senses.
> The **soul** makes us self conscious and gives us that awareness of our unique, individual identity.
> The **spirit** makes us God conscious enabling us to communicate with God thus making us unique amongst God's earthly creation.

Man is not the latest species in an endless evolutionary chain of development. He is the distinct and direct result of the purposeful work of God in a final act of creation. God concluded His work by producing Man, his masterpiece, in his own image and likeness. Man was created an eternal being and was appointed as God's representative over the rest of creation. (Genesis 2.19) The Psalmist writes that God has made man, 'to have dominion over the works of thy hands; thou hast put all things under his feet' (Psalm 8.6). Nevertheless all creation remains divine property on loan to man. (Psalm 50.10/11) The Lord Jesus, as Man, will one day rule on earth over all of God's creation (Daniel 7.14, 1 Corinthians 15.27, Ephesians 1.20-22, Philippians 2.9/10).

The rest of the Bible is taken up with God's relationship to man, not to other living or non-living things. We are God's greatest work, being capable of enjoying a personal relationship with God. The evolutionary scenario in which man arrives millions of years after the first living things, ignores God's main intention in creating man; indeed an evolutionary philosophy is incapable of arriving at such a conclusion for it operates at a relatively low level of understanding.

A diagram like this looks feasible and can be made to sound plausible but it is not scriptural. Man is distinct and unique over all God's creation. Adam was  not the son of a previous non-man, but as to his line of descent, he is described as 'of God' (Luke 3.38); having been formed by God directly from the dust of the earth (Genesis 2.7).

Within an evolutionary framework it could be argued that man is only a little superior to the animal creation but this is not taught in scripture. In Genesis 9.5/6 Noah was told by God of the distinction between the value of an animal's life and the value of a human life. The Lord Jesus also drew a clear distinction between the animal world and man by saying, 'you are of more value than many sparrows' (Matthew 10.31).

Evolutionary theory cannot account for the huge gap that exists between an ape and a human being who are, supposedly, closely linked in the chain of ascent. Man has capabilities far in excess of those needed simply to survive for he is able to carry out many more delicate and complicated tasks using superior levels of intelligence and learning that clearly determine his potential rather than simply being a response to a present need. The dexterity of his hands, the capacity of his memory and the range of sounds in his voice, including the sophistications of complex language, are clear examples. Evolution cannot explain how and why numerous languages should have developed when one is clearly more beneficial. The biblical explanation is found in Genesis 11.6/7.

The human brain has 10 million, million cells and 500 million, million connections that enable an amazing range of intellectual activity. Why should evolution 'require' the development of such highly complex material and what supposed pressures from natural selection existed to cause such abilities to evolve ? The biblical answer is plainly stated, that in making man distinct from all creation, God clearly had something special in mind for him. We are not simply advanced animals still in the process of an endless, purposeless, meaningless evolution. Sadly, so many fail to grasp this vital truth.

The word 'created' is used for the third time. It means to call into existence that which previously had no existence. It is used of the production of something that is fundamentally new and has never previously existed. This special work of God took place on three occasions.
1. When non-living matter was produced.
2. When living things were introduced with a physical consciousness of being.
3. When God brought in Man, a physical, but also a spiritual being.
In each case God produces an additional element that had not existed before. God also brings all subsequent life into being. Isaiah wrote, 'we are the clay, and thou our potter; and we are all the work of thy hand' (Isaiah 64.8).

Evolutionary theory has great difficulty in giving a satisfactory explanation for the co-existence of distinct male and female species which would have needed to evolve together in order to reproduce their own kind. God's record tells us they were there at the beginning

(Matthew 19.4), and did not arise as the result of many, many chance changes over millions of years. In Genesis 2.20 - 23 we learn that Adam did not have a helper who was compatible with himself amongst the animals, so God made a woman from the man to be a suitable companion. If evolution had occurred surely Adam's parents, brothers and sisters would have provided ideal companionship.

Population statistics provide strong evidence in support of the biblical view of human history. The present world population of 6,000 million people is consistent with a period of growth over 5,000 to 10,000 years. If man had been on earth for 50,000 years, which is much shorter than that claimed by evolutionists, the world would have reached saturation point long ago. Even at the lowest present growth rate the human population would now be hundreds of times greater. Amongst other questions, we have to ask why written records only go back several thousand years and why, if man has been around for 3 million years has he only recently made such technological advances? What has man been doing for around 2,995,000 years?

Adam was a perfect specimen, physically and mentally. He was highly intelligent, and possessed a perfect set of genetical information to pass on, as also did Eve, who became 'the mother of all living', (Genesis 3.20). Adam was ageless before sin came but the ageing and dying process began when sin intruded. God had warned Adam of the consequences of disobedience - 'dying thou shalt die' (Genesis 2.17). The full process of death took over 800 years, but it certainly came (Genesis 5.5).

Provision for all the variations in the human race were invested in the original genetic banks that God gave to Adam and Eve. Different traits have been manifested and brought out under different conditions (eg physical features). In early times there were fewer mistakes in the transmission of genetical information so that Cain and his brothers could marry their sisters. (Genesis 5.4) The passage of time has brought out many defects and diseases which are evidenced today, due to an increase in mutations, that is, mistakes in the copying and transferring of genetical material. Many of these mistakes have been brought on by man himself, as seen, for example, in atomic radiation.

God in His great wisdom has build in a mechanism that minimises naturally occurring genetical mistakes. The set of genetic instructions for the making of a human is about 3,000 million letters long, yet the actual rate of mistakes is in the region of 1 in 10,000 million. In the copying of these instructions there are some processes which are involved in the selection of the correct parts; others check or proof-read the selected material, removing incorrect information, and a third process repairs any mismatch which has slipped through the other two safeguards. The result is a marvellously accurate transmission of genetical information from one generation to the next, which maintains the stability of the distinctive 'kinds'. How great is our God and how foolish is man to think that numerous mistakes could even partly account for the huge variety of living things.

LESSON 11

Day 7 - COMPLETION AND REST

Genesis 2:1-3 'Thus the heavens and the earth were finished, and all the host of them. 2. And on the seventh day God ended his work which he had made; and he rested on the seventh day from all his work which he had made. 3. And God blessed the seventh day, and sanctified it: because that in it he had rested from all his work which God created and made.'

The first verse of chapter two takes us back to the first verse of the Bible in its mention of 'the heavens and the earth', and it confirms that the process begun there and continued through chapter one, now reaches its conclusion.

The first three verses of this chapter state three times that God had completed creating and making 'all' his work by day seven. It is confirmed in the New Testament that, 'the works were finished from the foundation of the world.' (Hebrews 4.3) This implies that the original creative work is complete and nothing more has been added to it. Present processes are not those of creation or innovation but of multiplication and conservation. As we have noted already, science can only deal with processes taking place today which are observable, measurable and repeatable.

The phrase 'host of them' refers to all the physical bodies in the heavens such as stars and planets. As previously mentioned, there is a possibility that it also includes angelic beings as in Luke 2.13.

On this final day of the week God rested in the enjoyment of a finished work and set this day aside as a special day. The Creator rested satisfied with the creation because it was precisely what He wanted it to be. This is the rest of completion not of tiredness. Isaiah wrote, 'Hast thou not known? hast thou not heard, that the everlasting God, the LORD, the Creator of the ends of the earth, fainteth not, neither is weary?' (Isaiah 40.28)

Other scriptures have much to say about the seventh day of rest, and these references confirm again that a literal interpretation of the Genesis record is correct. (eg. Hebrews 4.4,10) The fourth commandment (Exodus 20.8-10) stresses God's requirement of Israel to observe the Sabbath, the last day of the week. (See Exodus 23.12, Deuteronomy 5.14, Luke 23.56)

Reference has been made to the fact that early man would have been aware of the facts of creation from the records which were kept and handed down from generation to generation, but, like today, he chose to ignore these truths and to live according to his own inclinations. Such defiance against God led to very low levels of morality and to the further deterioration of the human race brought on by the infiltration of Satanic forces (Genesis 6.1-5). There is a strong indication here that men were possessed by demons in a similar way to that found in the gospels, where they are described as evil or unclean spirits which took control of humans, but only until they were confronted by the Lord Jesus Himself (Matthew 8.16, Mark 1.23-27, 5.2-13, Luke 7.21, 8.2).

God in His righteous judgement put an end to that evil humanity by sending a global flood. At the same time He displayed His grace by saving Noah and his immediate family, just as He does today for those who see their true condition before God and avail themselves of His great salvation (Romans 5.8).

The groups of people dispersed throughout the world following God's intervention at Babel (Genesis 11.8/9) would undoubtedly take with them detailed records of events from Adam to Noah together with details of the flood received from first hand witnesses, namely Shem, Ham and Japheth. As these families settled across the face of the earth, with many developing into tribes and nations, knowledge from these records would become corrupted by the influences of their own customs and folklore. Nevertheless numerous stories that have survived from different civilizations contain several features in common with the biblical narrative such as a man, a flood, a vessel and a bird, indicating a common origin of truth.

Chinese writing can be dated back to around 2230 BC following the dispersal of the nations at Babel (Genesis 11). These people developed pictograms to represent objects and by combining these were able to convey abstract concepts. The following diagrams give an idea as to how words were formed and they indicate that the early Chinese not only took a knowledge of creation and of the flood with them from Babel, but also built some of these events into their own language. Evidence of this nature speaks for itself and provides independent confirmation of the accuracy of the Genesis account, just as historical and archaeological documents and artefacts bear testimony to the reliability of the whole of scripture.

create

dust

+ life/motion

+ mouth/person

= speak

+ walk

= create

Spirit

heaven

+ cover

+ water

+ three
mouths/persons

+ worker of
magic

= Spirit

first

life

+ dust

+ man

= first

boat

vessel

+ eight

+ mouth/person

= boat

LESSON 12

IMPLICATIONS FOR BELIEF

Evolutionary thinking should not be considered in isolation from the general philosophies of men who live without God. Whilst those who accept evolution are not necessarily without standards for living, if evolution is believed to be taking place, then a logical argument can be made for man determining the rules of life without reference to the requirements of a Creator. If man is just a developing animal then a logical case could be made, for helping evolution along by rejecting people who are considered 'defective' or 'inferior' in any way. Rules about morality can be adapted to suit the conditions and pressures of the day. We can all form our own personal beliefs and create our own individual reality in which there are no absolutes, for one view is as valid as another. These are some of the awful but logical conclusions of an evolutionary theory built on random, chance existence and the struggle for survival.

In evolutionary theory sin is just an unavoidable part of the endless progress of man towards completeness. Each generation is just another link in an endless, meaningless, purposeless chain of life. Most significant of all, evolved man does not need a Saviour any more than he needed a Creator - he will make it on his own. The ultimate tragedy of atheistic evolutionism is that it robs man of God and of an understanding and enjoyment of all the great divine purposes for which God made us at the beginning.

The real issues of the creation/evolution debate are not those which appear on the surface. Today Christians usually seek to confront issues such as abortion, pornography, divorce, homosexuality and racism, but these are not the root issues, they are the logical outcome of a naturalistic belief system in which men determine the rules.

The Bible is the standard for all Christian thought; it is the Creator's manual, and God alone has the authority to set the rules which we ignore or meddle with at our own peril. As the human mind, educated or otherwise, gets further and further away from God, Christians need to strengthen their confidence in the accuracy and authority of scripture as the only reliable source of truth. Instead of simply addressing the symptoms we should be exposing the root cause which is man's rejection of God and of His Word as the only reliable explanation of life and the only reliable guide for living.

God's order is being altered by man bringing divine wrath upon the human race (Romans 1.18-32). It is to be expected that those who build on an evolutionary foundation will tamper with and try to improve on God's order, morally, spiritually and physically. The best results however, will always be obtained when we follow the Maker's instructions.

Error would undoubtedly fill more volumes than truth, in fact, truth is contained in one great volume, the Bible, which is the word of God. It is better and more positive to be well versed in that which is true than in that which is false. If we read our bibles prayerfully, carefully and continually our minds will be filled with those valuable things that God wants us to know about and we will learn to appreciate the purpose of life from a far higher viewpoint.

The Bible clearly presents not only the truth about origins but also about the entrance of sin into God's world and the devastation it has caused. The same great book also tells us of God's remedy for sin in that He sent His Son, the world's Creator, to be the world's Saviour. Every individual sinner who repents of his/her sin and turns in faith to God for salvation through Christ will be eternally forgiven and eternally saved (John 3.16; Romans 5.8; 6.23; 1 Timothy 1.15).

The process of creation closely parallels God's even greater work of salvation in which He takes a sinful man or woman and makes of them a 'new creation' in and through the Person and work of the Lord Jesus Christ. (2 Corinthians 5.17) In this work also, God is systematic and purposeful in His dealings with us from a sinful, unconverted state to one of completion and fullness in Christ. His purpose for us and in us was not complete on the day we trusted Him as Saviour for spiritual progress is expected as we learn more of Him through His word.

The PRINCIPLE of salvation is reflected in Day 1 in which light and the movement of the Holy Spirit is seen as an essential requirement for God to work. Man is in moral and spiritual darkness (Proverbs 4.19) because of sin, and God who is light (1 John 1.5) has moved towards us in grace. So a Christian is a person who has been 'called out of darkness' (1 Peter 2.9) and is no longer characterised by it (Ephesians 5.8, 1 Thessalonians 5.5). The distinction between that which belongs to spiritual darkness and to spiritual light is one that God clearly establishes and expects us to observe.

The PATHWAY of salvation is pictured in Day 2 for it involves a new spiritual discernment and understanding of things as God views them. There are things which belong to heaven and there are things which belong to earth. A division or separation is necessary between those who belong to Christ and those who do not. We are not required to live in isolation, for we share much in common with all men, neither are we, as Christians, exempt from the numerous problems of life, nevertheless our minds should be 'on things above not on things on the earth'. (Colossians 3.2) The Lord wants us to be distinctive and to live as unmistakable Christians. (2 Corinthians 6.14 - 18)

The PRODUCT of salvation is illustrated in Day 3 in which we see new life evidencing itself in fruit bearing. Living things grow and develop according to the laws within their make-up; what is unseen within will be manifested by what is seen without. God requires fruit, that is, spiritual results, from those who belong to Him (John 15. 1-5). The Holy Spirit resides within the Christian enabling him/her to produce the fruit expected of a person under the Spirit's control (Galatians 5.22/ 23).

The PROCLAMATION of salvation is pictured in Day 4, for we as Christians are to be bright lights in a dark world. The moon has no light of its own, it shines only as it reflects the far greater light of the sun. Our witness to a godless world is best demonstrated as we reflect the greatness and wonder of the Lord Jesus in our own lives. We are 'in the midst of a crooked and perverse generation among whom ye shine as lights in the world'. (Philippians 2.15)

The POWER of salvation is seen in Day 5 as creatures are enabled by God to live in their respective surroundings. It is through the indwelling power of the Spirit that we are able to live contrary to the natural pull of earth and to move against the world's currents and tide. God has provided all that is necessary for His people to live victorious lives in the everyday environment of a hostile world.

The PURPOSE of salvation is reflected in Day 6 in which God reaches His main goal - man produced in His own image. So likewise God works within His own in order to reproduce Christ-likeness in every one of us. (Philippians 1.6) Each day of our lives God patiently works to achieve this through the trials and difficulties that we deal with, the attitudes we demonstrate and the love we display.

The PERFECTION of salvation is illustrated in Day 7 the end of which is not mentioned. This corresponds to the time when we shall have entered fully into God's rest; when this life will be over and we shall be with Christ forever. We will have said goodbye to the toils and burdens of a sin-spoilt earth and will have entered into the fullness of God's perfect salvation.

Soon, very soon, the Lord Jesus Christ, God's Son, will return to remove His people from earth to heaven (John 14.2/3; Philippians 3.20/21; 1 Thessalonians 4.16/17). God, the righteous judge, will then deal with earth's ungodly inhabitants and this will culminate in the glorious appearing of Christ (2 Thessalonians 1.7-10) as King to reign on earth for 1000 years (Revelation 20.6) and to reclaim His own world from the gross mismanagement of man. Then, after the final judgement of Satan and his followers, Christ will reign forever (Revelation 20.10; Ephesians 1.9/10).

The great purposes of God, begun in Genesis 1 and seemingly taken off course by Satan and man, will then be fully realized, appreciated and enjoyed by all mankind.

It is our prayer that you will be challenged to face up to the very real issues presented in this course - the issues of origin, purpose and destiny, and that you will make a personal decision to believe God, to rely on His Word, to trust His Son for salvation and to make spiritual progress along the pathway that leads to eternal blessing.

WHAT DO YOU THINK?

....
....
....
....
....
....
....
....
....
....
....
....
....
....
....
....
....
....
....
....
....
....
....
....

WHAT DO YOU THINK?

....
....
....
....
....
....
....
....
....
....
....
....
....
....
....
....
....
....
....
....
....
....
....
....

Further Reading

The Bible - Psalms 8, 19.1-4, 104, 136.5-9, 148

Baker S. Bone of Contention, Evangelical Press, 1987

Batten D. (Ed) The Answers Book, Australia: Creation Science Foundation, 1999

*Campbell I. * A Case for Creation,* 1999 (available from the author at 27 Ferndale Ave, East Boldon, Tyne & Wear, England NE36 0TQ)

Ham K. The Lie, California: Creation-Life Publications, 1992

Morris H.M. The Genesis Record, Michigan: Baker Book House, 1976

Milton R. The Facts of Life, London: Corgi Books, 1992

Rosevear D. Creation Science, Chichester: New Wine Press, 1991

*Snelling A (Ed) * The Revised Quote Book,* Brisbane: Creation Science Foundation, 1990

* These two books contain numerous quotations which show that many scientists recognize there are serious problems with evolutionary theory.

Other Sources

The following organisations provide excellent material relating to the issues mentioned in this course.

Answers in Genesis. (www.AnswersInGenesis.org)
P.O.Box 5262, Leicester, England. LE2 3XU

Biblical Creation Society, (www.grace.org.uk/orgs/bcs.html)
P.O.Box 22, Rugby, England. CV22 7SY

Creation Science Movement (www.csm.org.uk)
P.O.Box 888, Portsmouth, England. PO6 2YD